Best Management Practices

TREE SUPPORT

and Sharon Lilly

Companion publication to ANSI A300 Part 3 (2006), Supplemental Support Systems

ISBN: 1–881956–58–X

International Society of **Arboriculture**

The ISA seal is a registered trademark.

Editorial Coordinators: Peggy Currid and Sharon Lilly
Text and Cover Composition by: Kathy Ashmore
Cover Designer: Donnie Merrit

International Society of Arboriculture
P.O. Box 3129
Champaign, IL 61826-3129
(217) 355-9411
www.isa-arbor.com
e-mail: isa-arbor.com

20 19 18 17 16 15 14 13 12 11 10 9 8 7 6 5 4 3 2 1
03-07/1000/PC

ACKNOWLEDGMENTS

Best Management Practices Review Committee

Don Blair–Sierra Moreno Mercantile, Mountain View, CA

Erk Brudi–Munich, Germany

Joe Bones–Bartlett Tree Expert Company, Exton, PA

Scott Cullen–Consulting Arborist, Greenwich, CT

Rose Epperson–West Coast Arborists, Inc., Anaheim, CA

Richard Herfurth–Bartlett Tree Expert Company, Hooksett, NH

Tom Dunlap–Canopy Tree Care, Robbinsdale, MN

William Graham–Morris Arboreteum, Philadelphia, PA

Larry Hall–The Care of Trees, Wheeling, IL

Richard Jones–Davey Tree Expert Company, Kent, OH

Dennis Ryan–University of Massachusetts, Amherst, MA

Torrey Young, The Care of Trees, Oakland, CA

Drawings and cover design by Donnie Merritt, Bartlett Tree Research Laboratories, Charlotte, NC. Propping drawings by Renee Keydoszius-Byrd. Other illustrations provided by the International Society of Arboriculture.

Table of Contents

Purpose

Professionals in the field of arboriculture established a committee to develop standards for tree maintenance to provide a more uniform level of service and to help ensure public safety. This committee, working under the auspices of the American National Standards Institute (ANSI), developed standards for pruning, fertilization, support systems, and other aspects of tree care. *ANSI A300, The American National Standard for Tree Care Operations—Tree, Shrub, and Other Woody Plant Maintenance—Standard Practices* was written to provide minimal performance standards for use in writing maintenance specifications.

The International Society of Arboriculture (ISA) developed companion publications known as Best Management Practices (BMP) to aid in the interpretation and implementation of ANSI A300 standards. These publications are intended as guides for practicing arborists, tree workers, their supervisors, and the people who employ their services. The authors recognize that all trees are unique living organisms and that not all practices will work in all trees, so contracts and specifications developed using this manual and the ANSI A300 standard should be written or reviewed by a knowledgeable arborist. Departures from the standard should be made with careful consideration of the objectives and with supporting rationale.

The *Best Management Practices for Tree Support Systems: Cabling, Bracing, Guying, and Propping* is the companion publication for the *ANSI A300 Part 3 (2006)—Tree, Shrub, and Other Woody Plant Maintenance—Standard Practices, Supplemental Support Systems.*

Introduction

Tree support systems are used to provide supplemental support to leaders, individual branches, and/or entire trees. Cables, braces, and guys provide supplemental support by limiting the movement of the branches, leader, or an entire tree. When a tree has a structural defect or condition that poses a high risk of failure, which may result in injury or property damage, a supplemental support system can often reduce the risk. However, not all potential hazards can be mitigated by the installation of a tree support system. It is essential that each tree carefully be examined by a qualified arborist prior to the specification for and installation of, any support system. The arborist needs to ensure that the system will achieve its objective of providing added support, without increasing the risk of tree failure by changing the dynamics of the tree.

While the system is being installed, the tree worker may find additional defects. These defects must be reported to a supervisor, the arborist, and/or the client. Often the additional defects will require more pruning or cables, or possibly removal of the entire tree.

The most common structural defect with a high risk of failure is a codominant stem, often referred to as a "V-crotch" or weak junction (Figure 1). Because of the lack of direct structural connections between codominant stems, they are structurally weaker compared to a single stem, especially if bark is included between the two or more stems. These junctions may break by pulling directly apart or by moving to the side (shearing).

Figure 1. Codominant stems have a high risk of failure, especially if there is included bark at the union.

Another common condition with a high risk of failure occurs with long, heavy, or "overextended," branches. Overextended branches are ones that are unusually long for the tree species, are horizontal or downward growing, or have the majority of their foliage concentrated at the end of the branch. Breakage of these branches may occur at the junction with the stem, or they may split due to tension forces on the top and compression forces on the bottom of the branch. Splits occur when there is heavy loading, such as from snow or ice, or during a strong wind (Figure 2). Cables are used to reduce the risk of breakage and/or to keep branches off the ground, above pedestrians' heads or away from structures.

A third defect is the weakly anchored tree. This condition exists when a tree is transplanted with a substandard root ball, has uprooted, has defective roots due to damage or decay, or has another condition that results in poor root anchorage. Guying systems may reduce the risk of failure in these situations.

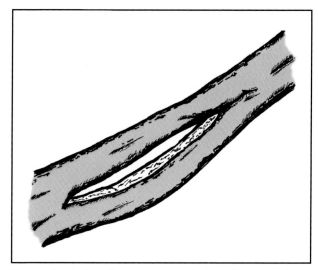

Figure 2. Limb split at the neutral plane between the compression and tension sides caused by an excess load.

In each of these cases, pruning or removal should also be considered. For young trees, pruning is the preferred method to eliminate codominant stems. The codominant stem may be removed entirely or it may be subordinated. Pruning may remove structural defects or lighten the load on tree parts with high risks of failure. On larger and mature trees, the combination of pruning and a support system may reduce the risk of failure. Removal is often the best remedy for trees with extensive decay, damaged root systems, or other critical risk conditions.

All support systems have a limited service life. Steel cables may last 20 to 40 years in an arid climate or with a slow-growing tree, but in an area exposed to salt spray or with a rapidly growing tree, cable service life could be much shorter. Less is known about the service life of fiber cable systems. Guy systems on newly transplanted small trees should be removed after one year unless a problem exists with the root system. On trees uprighted after storms or large transplants, guys should remain in place for three years or more until the root system re-establishes. On mature trees, guy systems may be required permanently. Their service life is similar to cables, and they will require replacement when worn or corroded.

Prior to installation of any tree support system, the client should be informed of the need for periodic inspection of the tree support system by a qualified arborist. The arborist should inspect the cable tension, condition of the cable and associated hardware, its height in the tree, and the structural integrity of the tree.

Support systems should be replaced or repaired when any of the following conditions are discovered:

- excessive wear, corrosion, or degradation of the system
- the tree has grown over the end of the cable or over a fabric cable sling
- tree growth has rendered the cable too low to be effective
- the cable has excessive slack
- the cable is rubbing against the tree
- anchors or terminations are substandard or no longer effective

Installation Tools

A wide selection of cables, braces, and hardware is used for tree support systems. The tools and materials used depend on the type of system, size of the tree to be supported, and the preference of the installer. Commonly used tools include the following:

Cable Aid

A cable aid is a device designed to turn lag hooks. It can also be used to aid in attaching dead-end grips (Figure 3).

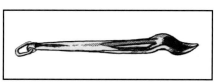

Figure 3. Cable aid used to turn lag hooks and attach dead-end grips.

Cable Puller

Cable pullers are used to temporarily attach a rope or come-along to a cable. There are two types of cable pullers: one for common-grade, galvanized cable, called a Haven grip, and one for extra-high-strength (EHS) cable, called a Chicago grip (Figure 4). The Haven grip slightly bends the cable, which could lead to premature failure if incorrectly

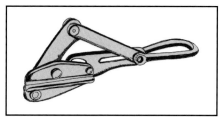

Figure 4. Chicago grip used to pull extra-high-strength (EHS) cable.

used on EHS cable. The Chicago grip pulls in a straight line, thus avoiding this problem.

Come-Along

When it is necessary to bring branches closer together, a rope or wire come-along can be used. A come-along is a manually operated, winch-type device. If a come-along is used, the bark should be protected, especially on thin-barked species in the spring.

Cutting Tools

Hacksaws are the recommended tool for cutting cables under tension, rods, and eye bolts. Bolt cutters or guy strand cutters are used to cut cables that are not under tension. Some guy strand cutters have a safety latch that fits over the cutting jaws to prevent user injury from the recoil of cut cable. Linesman's pliers are flat-tipped pliers used to bend individual cable strands when forming an eye splice and to cut off the excess portion of the strand after wrapping.

Drills

Four types of drills are used for installing support-system hardware: hand-powered braces, cordless electric drills, corded electric drills, and gasoline-powered drills. Braces are lightweight, durable, inexpensive, and dependable. They are preferred by some arborists for installing hardware in small and medium-sized branches.

Cordless electric drills, 18 volts or higher, do an excellent job of boring for lags and eye bolts. They are moderately priced and medium weight. Little maintenance is required, but spare batteries should be carried for unexpected failures.

Corded electric drills are heavier and require more setup time and a power source, but they provide much more drilling power and unlimited run time. Lag-threaded rods, up to the capacity of the drill chuck, can be fastened into the chuck of most drills and driven into the tree. High-torque electric drills usually have slower speeds to make this operation safer and easier. Higher-speed electric drills should not be used for large-diameter drilling or driving operations.

Electric cords need to be treated with great care to avoid accidental damage and potential electrical shock. Corded electric drills should be used in accordance with ANSI Z133.1 Safety Standards for Arboricultural Operations. Power cords need to be of sufficient capacity for the power draw (amperage) of the drill and the distance to the power source. Cords with insufficient capacity result in decreased drill torque, decreased drill motor life, and overloaded fuses or circuit breakers at the power source.

Gasoline-powered drills work well for many installations. Lag-threaded rods can also be fastened into the chuck of most gas drills and driven into the tree.

It may be preferable to independently suspend gasoline and corded electric drills in the tree when drilling long holes for brace rods so that the drill does not bend. Drills heavier than 15 pounds need to be tied into the tree on their own line, separately from the climber.

Drill Bits

Ship auger or wood auger drill bits are most commonly used for boring holes to install bolts or lags. Ship augers are designed to cut green wood; they have a single cutting edge and no cutting spur. They cut cleanly and quickly by rapidly removing chips through the hollow center (Figure 5). Single- and double-spur, solid-center augers are acceptable for smaller-diameter holes and relatively short drilling lengths

Figure 5. Ship auger drill bit used to drill live wood.

6

used to install lags or short bolts. Drill bits should be sharp; they will not cut straight if dull or damaged. For bracing, extremely long bits are often needed. Long bits or extensions can be purchased through arborist supply stores, or a steel rod can be welded onto the bit. Flat-spade bits, if slightly bent, will cut oversized holes that will affect the holding power of anchors. They are not recommended for arboricultural work.

Selection of the drill bit diameter depends on the type of anchor or rod, and wood characteristics. When installing machine-threaded rods, select a drill-bit diameter equal to or slightly greater than the rod diameter (Table 1). With lag-threaded hardware, the hole must be smaller than the hardware so the threads can "bite" into the wood.

Table 1. Recommended drill-bit sizes for dead-end (lag) and through bolts installed in most tree species.

Hardware diameter in inches	Diameter of the hole drilled in the tree, in inches, for	
	dead-end installation	through-bolt installation*
1/4	3/16	1/4
3/8	5/16	3/8 or 7/16
1/2	3/8	9/16 or 5/8
5/8	1/2	11/16 or 3/4
3/4	5/8	13/16 or 7/8
7/8	3/4 or 11/16	15/16 or 1
1	7/8 or 13/16	1-1/8

*With species, such as ash, that tend to close holes rapidly, use larger drill-bit size.
1 inch = 2.54 cm

Hammers

A ball peen or other hammer can be used to peen (deform) the last set of threads at the end of through-bolt hardware to prevent the nut from backing off.

Swage Tool

When forming eye splices in aircraft cables, metal swages are tightly clamped around the cable, using a large plier-like swage tool or Nico-press tool.

Tool Bucket or Bag

To hold the necessary tools aloft, a linesman's canvas tool bucket or other suitable lightweight bucket or bag is typically used.

Wrenches

Wrenches are used to turn nuts on all through-bolt installations. The wrench used can be an adjustable wrench or box wrenches of the correct size for the

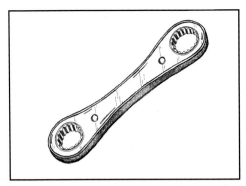

Figure 6. Ratchet wrench used to rapidly tighten nuts on long bolts or in confined spaces.

nuts. A ratchet wrench to allow rapid tightening of nuts in tight quarters (Figure 6) may be preferable for eye-bolt installation. A pipe wrench can be used for installing a lag-threaded, dead-end brace.

Hardware

Various pieces of hardware can be included in support systems. It is beneficial for the client and the tree if hardware is resistant to weathering. This means that steel hardware should be stainless, galvanized, or painted to reduce the potential for rusting. Fiber cables need to be treated to resist ultraviolet (UV) degradation; resistance to squirrel feeding is also beneficial. Wooden support used for propping should be treated to resist rotting.

Cabling

Cables restrict the distance that branches can move in relation to each other. Installed across a weak junction, they will greatly reduce the risk of failure. Installed on overextended branches, they can be used to support the branch. Because one cable will not necessarily protect a branch from twisting or shearing off at the junction, it is sometimes necessary to install more than one cable or a combination of cables and brace rods. Prior to installing a cable, the objective of the installation must be clearly defined.

Cable systems minimally consist of a set of anchors, a cable, and the appropriate means of termination or connecting the cable to the anchor. If the tree dictates a more complex system, more cables and/or brace rods may be required.

Location and Number of Cables

Cable anchors are installed about two-thirds the distance from the junction to the ends of the branches (Figure 7). Exact placement depends on the location of lateral branches and defects. Branches at the point of cable attachment must be large and solid enough to provide adequate support for the hardware. Installing cables farther from the junction can theoretically increase system strength, but much farther than two-thirds the distance might place cables in branches that are too small. When selecting the location for the anchors, avoid areas with decay, sharp bends, or other defects.

Installing the cable directly across the junction being supported will maximize support. The correct angle of the cable is perpendicular to an imaginary line that bisects the angle between the tree parts being cabled (Figure 8).

When selecting the number of cables, it is most important to look at the tree's needs rather than selecting a predesigned system type. With the simplest, most common case where cabling is

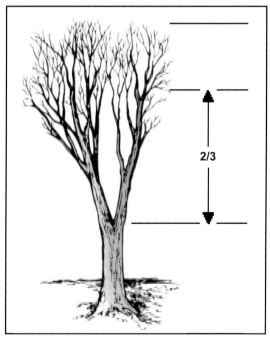

Figure 7. Cable anchors are installed two-thirds the distance from the junction to the ends of the branches. The placement depends on branch size and configuration.

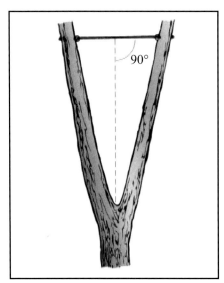

Figure 8. The cable should be installed perpendicular to an imaginary line that bisects the junction.

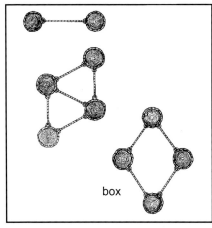

Figure 9. Configurations of commonly used cable systems.

required, two codominant stems are connected with a single, direct cable. If the junction has a split, decay, or other defect, the arborist should consider installing a brace in addition to the cable.

If more than two stems or branches require cables, more-complex systems may be required. The closer to directly across the junction the cables are installed, the less movement will be allowed in the junction, minimizing the chance of breakage. In addition to direct cables, other systems include triangular, box, and hub and spoke (Figure 9).

Triangular systems connect branches in groups of three. This method is applied when maximum direct support is required. Box systems can be used to connect four or more branches. This system provides minimal direct support, thus allowing more branch movement than with direct or triangular systems.

Hub-and-spoke systems consist of a centrally attached steel ring hub with cables radiating to three or more branches. They are used when there is no central leader to connect to. Hub-and-spoke systems lack lateral support and are difficult to install because the tension of each cable must be adjusted independently. All cables are installed taut (that is, with the minimum tension required to remove cable sag).

Anchors

Cables are anchored to branches with eye bolts, amon-eye nuts on threaded rods, lag hooks (J-lags), or lag eyes. Lags have less strength (Table 2), less holding power, and are restricted from use in decayed wood. Because of these limitations, eye bolts or threaded rods with amon-eye nuts are the preferred type of anchor for most cables (Figure 10).

Table 2. Approximate working-load limit (WLL)* of various components in tree support systems (in pounds).

Hardware diameter in inches	Eye bolts	Lag hooks	Amon-eye nuts	Common galvanized cable	EHS cable	Aircraft cable	Poly-propylene rope†	Polyester HMWPe‡	Turn-buckles	Compression springs
1/8				108		400				
3/16				230	798	840				
1/4	550	100	520	380	1330	1400				
5/16	850	200	840	640	2240	1960				890
3/8	1250	300	1240	850	3080	2880	220	(10/5) 1000	1040	1247
7/16			1700	1140	4160	3900		(10/20) 4000		1620
1/2	2250	600	2400	1480	5380	5000	880	(13/11) 2200	1960	2020
9/16						8000				
5/8	3600	900	3600				1760		3160	
7/8	7200	7200	7200							

*Working-load limit is defined as the breaking strength, as determined by the manufacturer, divided by a design factor. For this table, the design factor was assumed 5:1, or 20 percent, of the breaking strength.

†Cobra is constructed of polypropylene rope.

‡TreeSave is constructed of polyester or high-molecular-weight polyester (HMWPe) with or without a core. Shown in parentheses are TreeSave diameter (given in millimeters) and tensile strength (in 1000 pounds).

1 inch = 2.54 cm

Eye bolts should be drop forged rather than circular bent because of the higher strength of forged eyes. Eye bolts are installed in holes equal to or slightly larger than the bolt (Table 1). Using an eye bolt several inches longer than the diameter of the branch allows room for adjusting the tension of the cable. If a large-diameter anchor is installed in a small branch, there will be an increased chance of branch breakage. If too small of an anchor is installed, tension from the cable might break or pull out the anchor. Minimum and maximum sizes of branches for anchor installation are specified in Table 3.

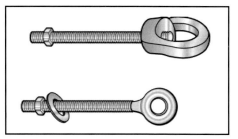

Figure 10. Threaded rod with amon-eye nut (top); eye bolt (bottom).

Eye bolts can be installed in decayed branches if the decay does not exceed 70 percent of the diameter of the branch at that point. The remaining 30 percent of sound wood should be nearly equally distributed around the branch. If the side of the branch where the nut will be attached has less than 15 percent sound wood thickness, another location in the tree should be found for anchoring the system. Branches or trunks with less than 30 percent sound wood are at a high risk to fail, so removal should be considered (Figure 11).

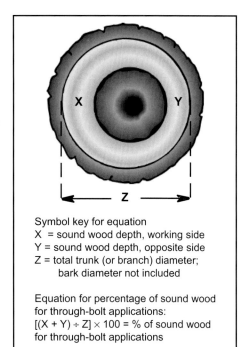

Symbol key for equation
X = sound wood depth, working side
Y = sound wood depth, opposite side
Z = total trunk (or branch) diameter;
    bark diameter not included

Equation for percentage of sound wood
for through-bolt applications:
$[(X + Y) \div Z] \times 100 = \%$ of sound wood
for through-bolt applications

Figure 11. Branches or trunks with less than 30 percent sound wood $[(X+Y) \div Z) \times 100)]$ should be considered for removal rather than cabled or braced.

When lag hooks are installed as cable anchors, a pilot hole must be drilled first. The hole should be slightly deeper than the lag's threaded portion and smaller in diameter than the lag (Table 1). If decay is encountered when drilling the pilot hole, a through anchor (eye bolt or threaded rod with amon-eye nut) should be installed, or the anchor site must be relocated to a decay-free site.

Lag hooks are available in right- and left-hand thread patterns (Figure 12). To have room for adjustment and to avoid unscrewing the other hook, one of each thread direction should be used on a cable. Lags must be used only when

Table 3. Minimum and maximum diameters of branches for eye-bolt installation.

Eye bolt diameter in inches	Minimum branch diameter in inches	Maximum branch diameter in inches	Maximum commonly available length in inches
1/4	1.5	5	4
5/16	2.0	8	4
3/8	2.25	18	6
1/2	3	24	18
5/8	3.75	28	24

1 inch = 2.54 cm

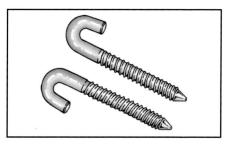

Figure 12. Left- and right-hand threaded lag hooks.

they can be seated to the full length of the threads without damaging the inner bark. This requirement may limit the use of lags when the installation is not perpendicular to the branch.

Anchor hardware must be installed in direct line with the cable (Figure 13). An off-center pull on anchors greatly reduces the strength of the anchor. To avoid bending the anchor, only one cable shall be attached to an anchor. When more than one anchor is installed in a branch, the anchors should not be installed directly above one another. Hardware should be installed either no closer together than the diameter of the branch (Figure 14), or with a separation of 12 inches (30 cm), whichever is less. These two means of anchor separation reduce the risk of wood splitting between the anchors.

Cables and Terminations

Two types of cable commonly are used for trees: common-grade (soft galvanized cable) and extra-high-strength (EHS) cable. While these two types of cable appear to be identical and weigh the same, there are major strength (Table 4) and bending differences. Cables are terminated (attached to the anchor

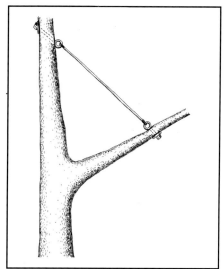

Figure 13. Anchor hardware must be installed in direct line with the cable to ensure maximum strength of the system.

13

Table 4. Minimum hardware size requirements for cabling trees (adapted from ANSI A300 Part 3, Table A-1).

Max. branch diameter at point of attachment in inches	Est. load in pounds	Lag-hook diameter in inches	Eye-bolt diameter in inches	Amon-eye threaded rod diameter in inches	Common-grade cable diameter in inches	Extra-high-strength cable diameter in inches	Aircraft-cable diameter in inches
2	100	1/4	1/4	1/4	1/8	3/16	1/8
3.5	200	5/16	1/4	1/4	3/16	3/16	1/8
5	300	3/8	1/4	1/4	1/4	3/16	1/8
8	600	1/2	5/16	5/16	5/16	3/16	3/16
10	900	5/8	3/8	3/8	3/8	1/4	1/4
15	1000	NA*	3/8	3/8	7/16	1/4	1/4
18	1200	NA	3/8	3/8	1/2	1/4	1/4
20	1400	NA	1/2	1/2	1/2	5/16	1/4
24	2200	NA	1/2	1/2	NA	5/16	3/8
28	3300	NA	5/8	5/8	NA	7/16	1/2
30	3700	NA	NA	7/8	NA	7/16	1/2

*Indicates that the application is not acceptable.
1 inch = 2.54 cm

hardware) with an eye that includes a heavy-duty thimble around the anchor (eye bolt, amon nut, or J-lag). The type of eye that is formed depends on the cable type. Manufactured dead-end cable terminations (fasteners hold the cable from the back side of the branch) are acceptable under the ANSI standards but are not well researched.

Common-grade (soft galvanized) cable is composed of seven strands of wire and is relatively easy to bend. It is terminated with an eye splice. To make the eye, the cable is wrapped around the thimble and bent parallel to the working side of the cable. One strand of cable is removed from the free end of the cable, close to the thimble. That strand is then wrapped tightly at least twice around both cables. There is no strength gain by wrapping more than twice around the cable. Any excess wire is cut off. The process is repeated with each strand, wrapped in the same direction, until all strands are wrapped (Figure 15).

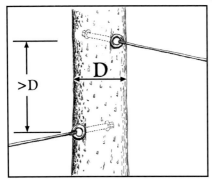

Figure 14. Hardware should be installed either no closer together than the diameter of the branch, or with a separation of 12 inches (30 cm), whichever is less.

EHS cable is composed of seven strands of galvanized wire. The cable is much stiffer than common-grade cable so it cannot be hand spliced. Instead, it is terminated with a manufactured dead-end grip. It is essential that the grip size match the cable size. The manufactured grip, including a heavy-duty thimble, is inserted through the anchor, and the

14

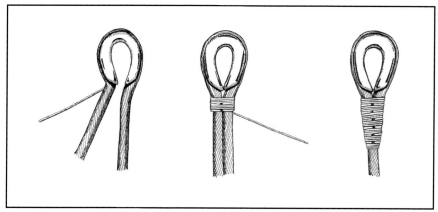

Figure 15. Common-grade galvanized cable is terminated with an eye splice that includes a thimble. The splice is made by wrapping each strand at least two times around all of the other strands. After wrapping, the excess wire is cut off. The process is continued until all of the strands have been wrapped.

short leg of the grip is wrapped around the cable (Figure 16). The long leg is then wrapped around both the cable and the other leg of the grip (Figure 17). It is essential that the last portion of the grip be locked into place around the cable. Dead-end grips cannot be shortened or altered in any way because doing so reduces the strength of the system. Prior to cutting EHS cable, apply tape around the cut site to prevent unraveling of the cable.

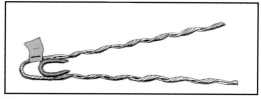

Figure 16. A thimble must be installed when using a dead-end grip.

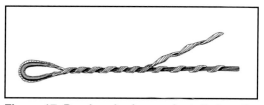

Figure 17. Dead-end grips are installed on the cable by wrapping the short leg of the grip around the cable, then wrapping the long leg. Both legs must be wrapped completely.

Aircraft cable, made of 19 strands of galvanized wire, can also be used in tree applications. This type of cable is strong and flexible (Table 4). Terminations are made using metal swages that are crimped tightly to the cable. Aircraft cable is terminated by sliding a swage of the proper size on the cable. The cable and thimble are inserted through the anchor and an eye is formed. The free end of the cable is inserted through the swage, then the swage is positioned close to the thimble and compressed (Figure 18). Excess cable is cut off, usually prior to fastening the swage.

Cable clamps (wire rope clamps, bulldog clamps) are not used in North America to form terminations on any cable larger than 1/8 inch (0.3 cm) diameter.

Figure 18. Aircraft cable is terminated with a thimble and a swage fastener. Insert the fastener over the cable, form the eye including the thimble, move the swage close to the thimble with the end of the cable extending past the swage, and finish the termination by crimping the swage with the proper tool.

They are commonly used in the United Kingdom and Australia, however. Cable can pull through cable clamps under repeated shock-loading when fewer than three clamps are used or if they are not properly installed. Wire-rope clamps are installed with the saddle side of the clamp against the longer section of cable. All three clamps are installed in the same orientation.

If compression springs are used in a cable system to reduce the speed of branch deceleration when the cable is tight, they must meet the same minimum strength requirements as the rest of the system hardware (Table 4).

Synthetic rope is used in proprietary sling cabling systems, such as the Cobra and the Osnabrück systems. The size of the line must meet the same minimum strength requirements as steel cable (Tables 2 and 4). These systems are treated to reduce the effects of ultraviolet (UV) light. They must be installed according to manufacturers' recommendations. Fiber systems need to be inspected frequently, because they tend to deteriorate from UV light exposure.

Thimbles

No matter what type of steel cable is used, a galvanized or stainless-steel thimble must be incorporated in the termination. The thimble reduces abrasive wear and increases the cable-bend radius. Heavy-duty thimbles must be used with EHS cable. These thimbles have deeper gullets as well as thicker steel.

The thimble should be left open with EHS cable so that the thimble cannot fall out of the dead-end grip. With common-grade galvanized and aircraft cable, thimbles should be closed after installing on the anchors.

Washers

Washers are used in all through-bolt applications to reduce the risk of the nut pulling through the tree. Washers should be heavy duty or heavy duty and heat treated. Heavy-duty washers are made of thicker metal than standard-duty washers and have a larger outside diameter. Heat-treated washers have even greater metal strength than heavy-duty washers.

Safety

To avoid potential electrical shock and be in compliance with ANSI Z133 safety standards, cables should not be installed over or within 10 feet (3 m) of energized electric wires.

When replacing cables, it is not always necessary to remove the old cable. However, if the client prefers removal of the old cable, the new cable must be installed first. Whether removing an old cable for replacement or for branch/tree removal, the tension should be removed from the cable before cutting the cable. Tension is removed using a come-along or other device. If a cable under tension must be cut, it should be cut with a hacksaw, not with a bolt or cable cutter. The tree worker must be in a position to avoid cable recoil or branch failure if they occur.

All leftover bits of cutoff wire, cable, and brace rod should be immediately collected and disposed of so as not to cause flat tires, personal injury, or lawn-mower damage.

Cables and Lightning

If a tree with a cable is struck by lightning, a higher likelihood exists for tree damage because the lightning can be conducted into the cambium and xylem. If there is a lightning protection system in a tree with a cable, the two systems should be connected (bonded) to reduce the risk of a lightning strike traveling between the two systems and causing tree damage. The connection should be made by fastening the lightning conductor to the cable with a specially designed bronze or stainless-steel connector clamp. Copper conductor should never be wrapped around the cable because galvanic corrosion will lead to premature cable rusting.

Bracing

Brace rods are used to reduce the risk of two or more leaders spreading farther apart or moving sideways in relation to each other. They are also used to fasten together a junction or branch that is split apart. When bracing trees, at least one cable is usually installed for added support. In cases where it is impractical to install cables, rods can be used alone, but the strength gain will be less than with a cable system. Prior to installing brace rods, the objective of the installation must be clearly defined.

There are two types of rod installations, through braces and dead-end braces. Through rods go entirely through the tree and are fastened at both ends with washers and nuts. Rods used for through bracing are machine-threaded or lag-threaded rod steel. Heavy-duty washers and nuts are used to fasten each end of the rod. If internal decay is present in a tree, only through braces can be used, and there must be a minimum thickness of sound wood of no less than 30 percent of the diameter of the tree at the point of installation (see Figure 11, p. 12).

Dead-end braces go entirely through the smaller of the two leaders and at least halfway into the larger leader. The rod used for dead-end braces is lag threaded to hold the wood without nuts. Solid, strong wood is needed for this system. Dead-end braces cannot be used if decay is present in the path of the rod, or if the tree is a poor compartmentalizer or has weak wood characteristics. Due to these limitations, through bracing is preferred for most bracing situations.

Table 5 specifies the minimum number and diameter of steel brace rods for various sizes of trees. When using this table, the tree diameter is measured below the junction being supported (Figure 19). Bronze rods can reduce the risk of injury if rods hidden within a piece of wood are sent through a chipper. Bronze rods will work in trees; however, the size requirements are known only for small trees. In these cases, 1/4-inch-diameter (0.6 cm) bronze rods can be used in junctions up to 4 inches in diameter.

Table 5. Minimum diameter and number of steel rods to install for bracing trees.

Diameter below the junction in inches	Brace-rod diameter in inches	Minimum number of rods in trees with	
		split limbs or included bark/split V-crotches	no split in the V-crotch
<5	1/4	1	1
5–8	3/8	1	1
8–14	1/2	2	1
14–20	5/8	2	1
20–40	3/4	3 + 1 for each 8" above 30"	2 + 1 for 8" above 30"
>40	7/8	4 + 1 for each 8" above 40"	3 + 1 for each 12" above 40"

1 inch = 2.54 cm

Rod Location

The preferred location for a single brace rod used to support a non-split junction is above the junction at a distance one to two times the diameter of the larger branch, measured above the junction. For example, if the larger leader is 18 inches (46 cm) in diameter above the junction, the brace rod should be installed 18 to 36 inches (46 to 91 cm) above the junction.

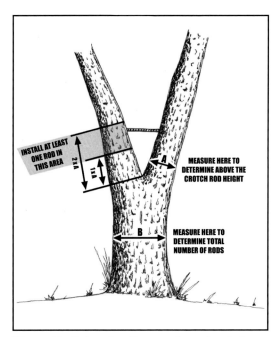

Figure 19. Determine the number of rods by measuring the diameter below the junction. Install at least one rod above the junction.

Bracing System Types

Commonly used bracing configurations include single rod, vertically parallel, horizontally parallel, alternating, and crossing. Tree size and defect determine which system is used.

On small trees, with a diameter of 8 inches (20 cm) or less, without a split below the junction, a single rod should be installed above the junction (Figure 20). With medium-sized trees [8 to 20 inches (20 to 51 cm) diameter] that have a split or large amounts of included bark below the junction, a vertically parallel system should be used (Figure 21). This includes one rod above the junction and at least one rod below the junction to pull the split together. The lowest rod should be no lower than the bottom of the split. Distance between rods should be equal to or greater than the diameter of the tree at the rod.

In larger trees, 20 to 40 inches (51 to 102 cm) in diameter, that have a single junction and a split below the junction, an alternating rod system should be used (Figure 22). This includes one rod above the junction and two or more rods below the junction that are horizontally offset from each other. Vertical distance between rods should be equal to or greater than the diameter of the tree at the rod, or 12 inches (30 cm) apart, whichever is less.

In very large trees, greater than 40 inches (102 cm) diameter, that have a single junction and a split below the junction, a horizontally parallel system should be used (Figure 23). This includes one or more rods above the junction and sets of horizontally parallel rods below the junction. Sets may consist of two or more rods spaced at least 12 inches (30 cm) apart, horizontally. If multiple rows of rods are used, vertical spacing should be at least 12 inches (30 cm).

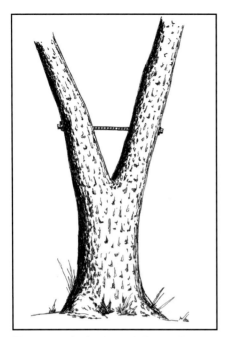

Figure 20. A single rod above the junction is the most commonly used bracing system.

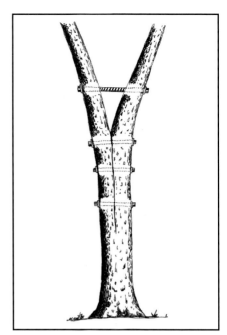

Figure 21. Vertically parallel rods are used in medium-sized trees with a long split or large amounts of included bark.

For trees with three or more codominant stems, a crossing system should be used (Figure 24). This includes one or more rods above the junction and two or more rods below the junction. Each stem should have at least one rod installed across the weak junction. Minimum horizontal rod spacing should be equal to or greater than the tree diameter at the rod, or 12 inches (30 cm) , whichever is less.

Installation Techniques

The hole for through-brace installation must be drilled completely through all sections of the tree to be braced (Figure 25). Never try to drill a hole from the opposite side of the tree because the holes will never directly meet.

To assist in closing a split junction, it may be necessary to install a come-along high above (where it will move the leaders at the junction but not bend them at the come-along) and draw the split together as much as possible before drilling the holes for the brace rod. If installing multiple rods, it is usually preferable to install the uppermost rod below the junction first.

Through Bracing

When using machine-threaded rods, the holes should be drilled equal to or larger than the diameter of the rod (see Table 1, p. 7). Machine-threaded rods

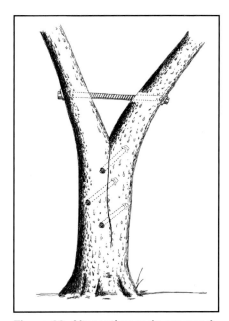

Figure 22. Alternating rods are used on large trees with a single junction and a large split below the junction. Rods are spaced at least 12 inches (30 cm) apart.

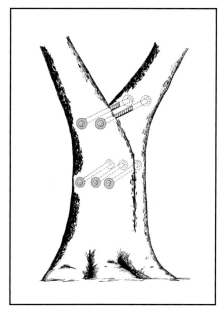

Figure 23. Horizontally parallel rods are installed on very large trees that have a split junction or large amounts of included bark. Two rows of rods, and at least one rod above the junction, may be used.

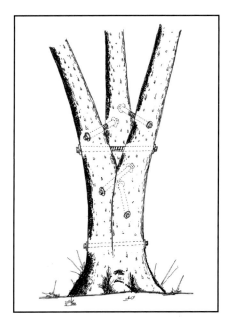

Figure 24. Crossing rods are used in large trees with more than one junction. At least one rod should support each major junction.

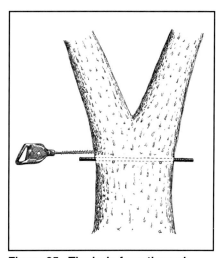

Figure 25. The hole for a through brace should be drilled entirely through all sections of the tree to be braced.

are terminated with heavy-duty washers and nuts. Nuts must be secured so that they will not back off of the rod. There are at least three options for securing the nut. A hammer can be used to peen at least one exposed thread toward the nut. Another method is to drill a hole through the nut and rod, and insert a wire wrapped around itself to lock the nut in place. Other alternatives include installing a locking nut or using locking fluid (Figure 26). Peening is the common method of securing a nut because it is inexpensive and has the benefit of not leaving a sharp, exposed edge.

With the rod fully inserted through the tree, a nut is fastened over a heavy-duty washer and tightened so that one or two threads are exposed for peening. On the opposite side, the washer is installed and the nut tightened to close the crack or secure the junction. Once tight, the excess rod can be cut off with a hacksaw and the nut secured.

On trees with thick bark, the bark should be removed to the sapwood beneath each washer. This procedure is known as countersinking. Without countersinking, the bark will compress, allowing movement of the washer and nut, possibly reopening the crack. Because of the increased potential for decay, countersinks should not go into the wood. On trees with thin bark, countersinking is not required.

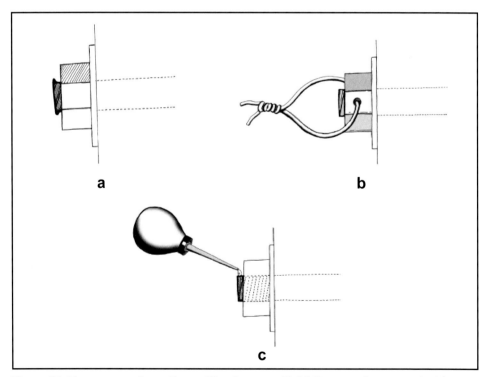

a

b

c

Figure 26. To secure nuts so they will not come off, (a) they can be peened with a hammer, (b) secured with a locking wire, (c) or fastened with locking fluid.

There are two accepted methods of countersinking. The preferred method is using a flat-bottom drill bit, such as a Forstner drill bit, of the same diameter as the washer (Figure 27). This bit produces a flat surface for the washer to rest on and very smoothly cut sides that result in faster closure than chisel-cut countersinks. It is easier to drill the countersink before starting the hole for the rod. On the opposite side, the countersink is drilled after the drill bit emerges from the tree.

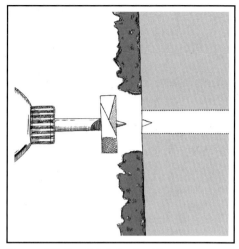

Figure 27. On thick-barked trees, countersinking the washer and nut can reduce movement. Only the bark should be countersunk; do not cut into the wood. Countersinking can be done using a flat-bottomed, Forstner drill bit or a chisel.

Chisels or gouges can also be used to cut countersinks. A gouge curved with the same radius as the washer is preferred. After the hole is drilled, the outline of the washer should be scribed to show where to chisel out the bark. Avoid damaging the bark outside of the scribed area.

With rods that will be partially exposed between stems, the exposed portion of the rod may be painted or covered with PVC conduit, if desired. The conduit may provide some protection against the weather, and it can protect children and climbing lines from being cut by sharp threads. Nuts, washers, and rod ends do not need to be treated with paint or asphalt sealant except for aesthetic reasons or in areas exposed to high levels of corrosion.

Dead-End Bracing

To install dead-end braces, drill the hole smaller than the rod (see Table 1, p. 7) entirely through the smaller stem and at least halfway into the larger stem (Figure 28). It may be useful to mark the drill bit and rod with tape before drilling so that it will be obvious when the proper depth is reached. This is done by holding the bit next to the tree and estimating the length required.

Lag-threaded rods are driven into the tree using a pipe wrench, drill, or rod driver. If using a pipe wrench, avoid damaging the rod if a nut will be attached. If using a drill, fasten the end of the rod in the chuck and drive it in at a slow speed. With any of the driving techniques, the job can be made easier if the rod is lubricated with silicone spray or soap.

If a nut is not used to secure the exposed end of a dead-end installation, break off the rod below the bark of the tree. This is done by driving the rod in most of the way, then sawing through the rod approximately two-thirds to three-quarters of the diameter of the rod, then carefully driving the rod in so that the precut portion is below the bark. The rod is then bent until it breaks at the cut.

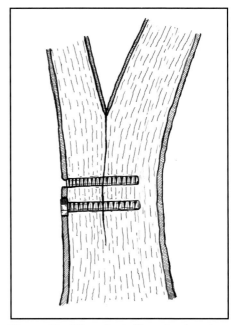

Figure 28. When installing dead-end bracing, drill entirely through the smaller stem and at least halfway through the larger stem.

Guying Established Trees

Guying is the installation of a cable between a tree and an external anchor to provide supplemental support and reduce tree movement. Although established trees are rarely guyed, there are a few cases where guys are installed. Trees that have been uprighted after being blown over may require support until their root system is re-established. Trees with serious root defects and that cannot be removed due to historic importance or other reasons may require guying to keep them upright or to prevent failure in the direction of a target. Prior to installing a guy system, the objective of the installation must be clearly defined, and the system needs to be designed to achieve this objective.

Public safety can be a concern when guying trees. It is important to notify the client of the risks involved with guyed trees. Guy systems might fail under extreme conditions. The client also must be informed of the need for periodic inspections of the tree and guys. Inspection intervals depend on the specific tree, site, and guy conditions. If defects are found in the tree or guy system, they must be corrected in a timely way to prevent damage.

Established tree-guying systems consist of an attachment point in the tree, the guy cable, and an anchor. Two types of anchors are common—soil anchors and other trees used as anchors.

The attachment point in the tree consists of lag hooks or through bolts. The size and installation considerations for these anchors are detailed in the Cabling section. Table 4 details the minimum hardware requirements. Permanent guy cables should not be wrapped around the tree.

 Tree anchors should be attached at a point not less than half the height of the tree. To avoid splitting the wood, multiple anchors must be separated by a distance not less than the diameter of the tree at the point of attachment.

With tree-to-ground guy systems, the size of the ground anchor is very important. It must have sufficient strength, even under wet conditions, to support the tree. When selecting an anchor, use either products specifically designed for the task or consult an engineer to aid in anchor design.

The ground anchor should be placed no closer to the tree trunk than two-thirds the distance from the ground to point of attachment on the tree. For example, if the lowest guy attachment on the tree is 24 feet (7 m) from the ground, the ground anchor should not be closer to the trunk than 16 feet (5 m) (Figure 29). Preferably, the distance from the tree should be nearly equal to the height of attachment in the tree.

Turnbuckles or compression springs used to adjust cable tension in a guying system must meet the same strength requirements as the rest of the system (see Table 4, p. 14).

Installing the ground anchor and guy cable within the mulched area around the tree will protect it from lawn-mower damage better than if the anchoring system is in a turf area. If guys are in an area that has pedestrian or vehicular traffic, they must be clearly marked or protected with flagging, PVC pipe, or other means. The client needs to be informed of the potential risk to pedestrians from the guy.

In tree-to-tree guy systems, other trees are used as anchors. When selecting an anchor tree, the tree must be carefully inspected to make sure that it has the structural strength to support the other tree. Trees with root damage or extensive decay should not be used as anchors. It is preferable that the anchor tree be larger than the guyed tree. Lags or eye bolts attached to the anchor tree must be the same size or larger than the hardware on the guyed tree. They must be attached on the lower half of the trunk, preferably at a height greater than 7 feet (2 m) off the ground if there is pedestrian traffic, or greater than 14 feet (4 m) off the ground if there is vehicular traffic under the guy cable (Figure 30).

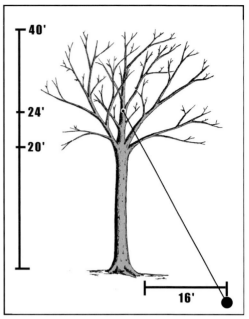

Figure 29. The preferred location of the ground anchor is the same distance out from the trunk as the height of the other end in the tree [in this case, 24 feet (7 m)]. The minimum distance is two-thirds the height [in this case,16 feet (5 m)].

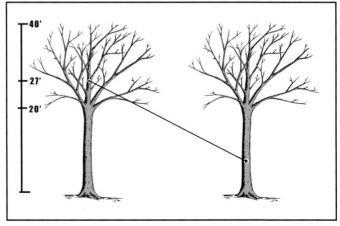

Figure 30. With tree-to-tree guys, the anchor should be installed at half of the tree height or higher on the anchor tree. The guy should be installed at least 7 feet (2 m) above the ground in areas with pedestrian traffic or 14 feet (4 m) above the ground in areas with vehicular traffic.

26

Propping

Props are rigid structures built on the ground that support a branch or trunk. Props are used under branches or leaning trunks to keep the branch off the ground or a structure or to provide clearance. Typically, props are used under branches that are nearly horizontal or growing downward.

Little information about the use or design of props in arboriculture is available, and there are wide variations in design. A key facet of any prop design is that it will not restrict growth of the branch.

Props can be made from wood, steel, concrete, or other materials. They must have sufficient strength to support the expected load. Green wood typically weighs 50 to 80 pounds per cubic foot (800 to 1,280 kg per cubic m), depending on tree species. The load should be expected to be greater if the trunk also leans toward the branch. Props constructed from wood and steel should be protected from deterioration caused by decay or rust.

The prop must have a provision to keep the branch from falling off. Options for keeping the branch on the prop include a pin, saddle, or bolt (Figures 31, 32, 33, and 34). The prop should be designed so as not to restrict growth of the branch. Saddles and straps have been used in the past, but they often end up damaging the branch by girdling; therefore, they should be avoided or adjusted frequently.

The prop must be anchored in the ground so as to keep it from moving excessively. If a hole is dug for this footing, root damage beyond the scope of the work must be avoided. A concrete footing is often the preferred anchor. It should be large enough to hold the expected load and deep enough to avoid frost heaving.

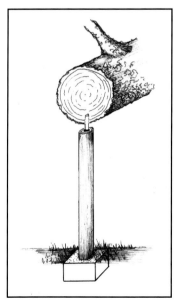

Figure 31. Basic prop designed for the branch to rest on a pin or bolt. Useful when side forces and trunk twisting will be minimal. Depth of foundation should consider load and frost-free depth.

Figure 32. Prop design used to minimize the effects of side forces. The branch rests on a pin or bolt.

Figure 33. Prop design used to minimize the effects of side loading and to allow some movement of the branch. This design is more difficult to construct and assemble on the tree. Can be installed only with an eye bolt or amon eye.

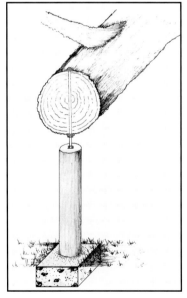

Figure 34. Through-bolt propping can be used instead of resting a branch on a pin when upward forces are anticipated.

Guying Newly Planted Trees

Staking, guying, and bracing are methods for mechanically supporting the trunk of a planted tree to keep it in an upright position. Staking is expensive and time consuming and may present a hazard because people could trip on the supports. Staking too rigidly can reduce trunk taper development on very small trees. The trunk taper of larger-sized trees typically planted in landscapes, however, is not often affected by staking.

Bare-root trees, as well as fabric-bag and container-grown trees with small, lightweight root balls, may require support until lateral or anchor roots develop. Large evergreens may need to be guyed because of the high wind resistance of the foliage and extra weight of snow and ice accumulation during the winter. Locations with persistent or strong winds or other unusual circumstances may require more frequent use of stakes. Do not use a support system unless it is necessary, and, in most cases, supports should be removed after one year to avoid trunk girdling.

Low guying can keep the tree in place while permitting the top to move freely. Attaching the guys above two-thirds the height of the tree can cause the trunk to break where the trunk bends sharply in the wind at the attachment point.

Two stakes, with separate flexible ties, usually are recommended. It is often easier to install stakes before the hole is backfilled. Guy wires and ground anchors are used on larger trees. Turnbuckles can be installed to make adjustments in length as needed. Compression springs can provide flexibility for trunk movement.

The traditional material for guying trees to stakes is a wire slipped through a piece of garden hose, but this method sometimes can cause damage. Guying material should be wide, smooth, nonabrasive, flexible, and, if possible, photodegradable. Table 6 contains examples of minimum material requirements for tree guys.

To prevent injury to the bark, the guying should be examined at least once during the growing season and adjusted if necessary.

Underground anchoring systems are sometimes necessary for aesthetic or safety reasons. An untreated wood frame held in place with underground guys will rot away in a few years after it is no longer needed. Other homemade and commercially manufactured root ball anchor systems also are available. Care should be taken not to use a system that requires additional soil to be placed over the root ball to cover it. All trees eventually have to be removed; therefore, the possibility of future damage to stump- grinding machines and injury to operators should be considered when using steel ground anchors or cables.

Table 6. Examples of minimum material requirements for tree guys (source: E. Thomas Smiley, Bartlett Tree Research Laboratory).

Maximum tree caliper (inches)	Minimum working strength (pounds)	Polypropylene rope (inches)	Steel wire Class I galvanized (gauge)	Soft galvanized cable 1 × 7 (inches)	Aircraft cable, galvanized 7 × 19 (inches)
1.5	75	3/16	16		1/16
2.5	100	1/4	16	1/8	1/16
4	180	5/16	14	3/16	3/32
6	320	3/8	12	1/4	1/8
8	640	NA	NA	5/16	3/16

1 inch = 2.54 cm

Glossary of Terms

amon-eye nut–a drop-forged eye nut used to fashion a through-hardware anchor.

anchor–hardware to which the cable termination is affixed in a cabling or guying installation.

anchor tree–a tree used to provide supplemental support in a guying installation.

arborist–a professional who possesses the technical competence through experience and related training to provide for or supervise the management of trees and other woody plants in the residential, commercial, and public landscapes.

bond–an electrical connection between an electrically conductive object and a component of a lightning protection system that is intended to significantly reduce potential differences created by lightning currents.

bracing–the installation of lag-threaded screws or threaded-steel rods in limbs, leaders, or trunks to provide supplemental support.

cable–(1) Zinc-coated strand per ASTM A-475 for dead-end grip applications. (2) Wire rope or strand for general application. (3) Synthetic-fiber rope or synthetic-fiber webbing for general applications.

cabling–the installation of a cable within a tree between limbs or leaders to limit movement and provide supplemental support.

compartmentalization–physiological process that creates the chemical and physical boundaries that act to limit the spread of disease and decay organisms.

dead-end brace–a brace formed by threading a lag-threaded screw rod directly into a limb, leader, or trunk but not through the side opposite the installation.

dead-end grip–a manufactured wire wrap designed to form a termination in the end of a 1×7 left-hand lay cable that meets the specifications of ASTM A-475 for a zinc-coated strand.

dead-end hardware–anchors or braces that are threaded directly into the tree but not through the side opposite the installation. Dead-end hardware includes but is not limited to lag hooks, lag eyes, and lag-threaded screw rods.

eye bolt–a drop-forged, closed-eye bolt.

eye splice–a closed-eye termination formed into common-grade cable by bending it back on itself and winding each wire around the cable a minimum of two complete turns.

grip–a mechanical device that grasps and holds a cable during installation.

connector clamp–a multipurpose bolt clamp that is used to bond conductors, or bond a conductor to a ground terminal or tree support system, and that meets the specifications of ANSI/UL-96.

guying–the installation of a steel cable of synthetic-fiber cable system between a tree and an external anchor to provide supplemental support.

lag eye–lag-threaded, drop-forged, closed-eye anchor.

lag hook (J-hook)–lag-threaded, J-shaped anchor.

lag-threaded hardware–anchors or braces with lag threads. Lag-threaded hardware includes but is not limited to lag eyes, lag hooks, and lag-threaded screw rods.

lag-threaded screw rod–lag-threaded steel rod, used for dead-end and through-brace installations.

peen–the act of bending, rounding, or flattening the fastening end of through hardware for the purpose of preventing a nut from "backing off."

qualified tree worker, person, or personnel–a person who through related training and on-the-job experience is familiar with the hazards of pruning, trimming, repairing, maintaining, or removing trees and with the equipment used in such operations, and who has demonstrated ability in the performance of the special techniques involved.

shall–as used in the ANSI standards, denotes a mandatory requirement.

should–as used in the ANSI standards, denotes an advisory recommendation.

taut–tightened to the point of eliminating visible slack.

termination–a devise or configuration that secures the end of a cable to the anchor in a cabling or guying installation.

termination hardware–hardware used to form a termination. Termination hardware includes but is not limited to dead-end grips, thimbles used in eye splices, and swages.

thimble–an oblong galvanized or stainless-steel fitting with flared margins and an open-ended base.

threaded-steel rod–a machine-threaded steel rod used for through-brace installations.

through brace–a brace formed by installing through-brace hardware into a limb, leader, or trunk, secured with nuts and heavy-duty washers. Through hardware includes but is not limited to eye bolts, lag-threaded screw rods, and threaded steel rods.

turnbuckle–a drop-forged, closed-eye device for adjusting cable tension.

wire rope clamp–a clamp consisting of a U-bolt, bracing plate, and fastening nuts.

Selected References

Blair, D.F. 1995. *Arborist Equipment: A Guide to the Tools and Equipment of Tree Maintenance and Removal* (2nd edition). International Society of Arboriculture, Champaign, IL. 300 pp.

Harris, W.H., J.R. Clark, and N.P. Matheny. 1999. *Arboriculture: Integrated Management of Landscape Trees, Shrubs, and Vines* (3rd edition). Prentice Hall, Upper Saddle River, NJ. 687 pp.

Shigo, A.L., and R. Felix. 1980. Cabling and Bracing. *Journal of Arboriculture* 6(1):5–9.

Smiley, E.T., 1998. Countersinking for tree bolts. *Journal of Arboriculture* 24(5):245–247.

Smiley, E.T., C.M. Greco, and J.G. Williams. 2000. Brace rods for codominant stems: Installation location and breaking strength. *Journal of Arboriculture* 26(3):170–176.

Stobbe, H., D. Dujesiefken, and K. Schroder. 2000. Tree crown stabilization with the double-belt system Osnabrück. *Journal of Arboriculture* 26(5):270–273.

Thompson, A.R. 1959. Tree Bracing. *Tree Preservation Bulletin No. 3*. National Park Service. U.S. Government Printing Office. 21 pp.

Tree Care Industry Association. *American National Standard for Tree Care Operations—Tree, Shrub, and Other Woody Plant Maintenance—Standard Practices (Support Systems a. Cabling, Bracing, and Guying* (A300, Part 3). Tree Care Industry Association, Manchester, NH.

Watson, G., and E.B. Himelick. 2005. *Best Management Practices: Tree Planting.* International Society of Arboriculture, Champaign, IL. 41 pp.

About the Authors

E. Thomas Smiley, Ph.D., is an arboricultural researcher at the Bartlett Tree Research Laboratories. He serves as technical advisor for the ANSI A300 Standards for Tree Care Operations and is chair of the ISA Best Management Practices Committee. He received his Ph.D. from Michigan State University, M.S. from Colorado State University, and B.S. from the University of Wisconsin–Madison.

Sharon Lilly is Director of Publications for ISA. She received her B.S. and M.S. from The Ohio State University and has more than 25 years of experience as a practicing arborist. Sharon is the author of many books, articles, and training manuals in the field of arboriculture.